Strike a Pose

written by **Karen Birkemoe** ✱ illustrated by **Heather Collett**

Kids Can Press

For my mom, my first ▮▮▮▮▮▮▮▮▮▮ o yoga
classes when I was only ▮▮▮▮▮▮▮▮ anidhiji,
with thanks for ▮▮▮▮▮▮▮▮▮▮

Thanks to Stacey Roderick and Valerie Hussey for believing a book like
this was a good idea and for letting me do it. Thanks also to Karen Powers, Yvette Ghione
and especially Heather Collett for working tirelessly to make it just right. — KB

For my sister, Katie — HC

pLanet girL™ is a trademark of Kids Can Press Ltd.

Published in Canada by
Kids Can Press Ltd.
29 Birch Avenue
Toronto, ON M4V 1E2

Published in the U.S. by
Kids Can Press Ltd.
2250 Military Road
Tonawanda, NY 14150

www.kidscanpress.com

Edited by Stacey Roderick and Yvette Ghione
Designed by Karen Powers
Printed and bound in China

CM 07 0 9 8 7 6 5 4 3 2 1

Kids Can Press acknowledges the financial support of
the Government of Ontario, through the Ontario Media
Development Corporation's Ontario Book Initiative,
and the Government of Canada, through the BPIDP, for
our publishing activity.

Library and Archives Canada Cataloguing in
Publication

Birkemoe, Karen, 1974–
   Strike a pose : the planet girl guide to yoga / written
   by Karen Birkemoe ; illustrated by Heather Collett.

(Planet girl)
ISBN-13: 978-1-55337-004-8   ISBN-10: 1-55337-004-X

1. Hatha yoga—Juvenile literature. 2. Girls—Health
and hygiene—Juvenile literature. I. Collett, Heather,
1974– II. Title. III. Series.

RA781.7.B57 2007   j613.7'04608352   C2006-902911-3

Kids Can Press is a lorus™ Entertainment company

Contents

WHY DO YOGA?

Movie stars, athletes, musicians, scientists — it seems like everybody's doing yoga these days. And not one to just follow the crowd, you're probably wondering why.

This "health craze" has actually been around for thousands of years. In fact, the word yoga means "union" in the ancient language Sanskrit. Translation: Yoga means bringing together your body, mind and breath. How does this work? By showing you how to focus on your breathing, concentrate on your body's movements and stay in the moment. When your body, mind and breath are working together, you're relaxed and focused and everything gets easier.

Believe it or not, whatever you do, yoga can help you do it better. Nervous about standing in front of your class to give a report? Find a quiet corner for a few simple yoga poses, and *hello*, confidence.

$e = mc^2$

So stressed you can't sleep? Learn to chill out without late-night TV just by breathing a certain way. Want to get better at your favorite sport and stay injury free? Check out the Yoga For All You Are and Do section (page 70). Just hanging around the house? The DIY Yogini section (page 82) shows you how to make some cool stuff for your yoga practice and how to really pamper yourself and your friends.

Hatha yoga, the yoga that's described in this book, is the most popular physical yoga practiced today. Anyone can do it and feel fantastic as a result, even those of us with physical challenges. To start doing Hatha yoga, it's much more important to have an open mind than a flexible body. Strength and flexibility happen in time and with practice.

Once you give it a try, you'll find your own reasons for doing yoga. It isn't something to just read about — you need to try it to get the most out of it. This book has all the info you need to get started, so as you read along, experiment, laugh, breathe and see where yoga takes you.

WHERE DID YOGA COME FROM?

THE MYTH

The story goes like this: A boy was born on an unlucky day, so his parents threw him in the river, where he was swallowed by a fish. Hidden in the fish, he overheard Lord Shiva (a Hindu god) explaining all the yoga poses and secrets to his wife, Parvati (a Hindu goddess). Eventually the boy went on to spread the yogic teachings to the human race.

THE FACTS

The first signs of yoga poses show up in 5000-year-old artifacts from the Indus Valley in northwestern Pakistan. Not everyone agrees on who invented yoga because it is practiced in many different cultures, which isn't that surprising since yogis traveled and shared what they knew. Yogic wisdom is also found in ancient texts like the *Yoga Sutras of Patanjali*, which discusses yogic philosophy, and the *Hatha Yoga Pradipika*, which describes how to do physical yogic practice.

What changed over the years were the reasons for doing yoga. For a time it was believed to be a path to spiritual enlightenment. At other times it was considered simply a way to live longer, more healthily and happily.

It's been fewer than 200 years since yoga came to North America and Europe, and now there are more people on the planet practicing yoga than ever before. That's because yoga isn't about wandering off into the mountains to find a guru to teach you to commune with your higher self. It's about seeing how this ancient practice can fit into your modern-girl life, making it better than it was before.

READ ME FIRST: Gettin' it right

Here's what every yogini (that's you) needs to know before starting her yogic practice.

WHEN?

Having an empty stomach is key. Try practicing in the morning before your hit of O.J. or in the early evening before you chow down on dinner.

HOW OFTEN AND HOW LONG?

These are great questions, but ones you'll have to work out for yourself. Keep in mind that

- ⊙ yoga should never wear you out — you shouldn't need even a day to recover

- ⊙ the more regularly you practice, the more you'll benefit

- ⊙ 15 minutes of yoga is better than no yoga at all, so do what you can

Order vs. Chaos

Each of the two sections on asanas, or poses, is set up in a particular sequence, or order, just like your own personal yoga class. Try to follow the sequence of the asanas to avoid injuries and to get the most out of your practice. Both sections follow the same format: forward bends, back bends, side bends, twists, balances, inversions, seated poses and relaxation.

After the sequence sets, do some pranayama, or breathing exercises (page 62), and then meditation (page 66). Even if you are as bendy as an elastic band, begin with the Getting Started section (page 14). These poses are the building blocks you'll need for the more advanced ones. When you can do all the poses easily, move on to the Going Further section (page 32).

The steps

Before trying an asana, read the instructions through a few times. Then string the steps together as you try the pose. (If you're with a friend, try reading out the instructions for each other.) With practice, you will flow in and out of the poses naturally.

Some poses work your whole body equally, but you'll have to do most poses on each side of the body to keep yourself balanced. Count your breaths on the first side and then take the same number of breaths on the other to work both sides equally.

Repetitions

At the end of each pose there are suggestions for how long to hold it and how many times to repeat it. If you have the time, try the suggested number of repetitions or hold the pose longer. If you're short on time, you may only have time to do the pose once on each side.

Breathing

Your breathing is just as important as the movements and poses. Using your breath is the secret key to getting your body, mind and breath to really connect. Try it and you'll see.

Unless the instructions say otherwise, always breathe in and out through your nose. This warms and cleans the air you breathe. The instructions also tell you which movements to breathe in on and which movements to breathe out on. And counting your breaths in the poses will make you more aware of your body and help keep you focused.

R&R

Rest and relaxation are also important parts of yogic practice. The relaxation asana called the Corpse pose (page 30) is super important. Try it between each pose if you like, but definitely do it at the end of your sequence to soak up all the benefits of your efforts and to let go of any leftover tension.

Pain is a four-letter word

Nothing in this book should ever hurt. This is very important to remember. Straining or pushing too hard in a yoga pose is a surefire way to hurt yourself, and recovering from an injury always takes longer than you'd like. So listen to your body! If you're having trouble breathing in a pose, or the parts you're stretching burn or feel like they're going to rip apart, guess what? You're overdoing it! Give yourself a break and change your approach. The world isn't going to stop if your head doesn't touch your knees.

Yoga will help you accomplish things you might never have thought possible, both physically and in other areas of your life. But this won't happen overnight or even after a week of daily yoga sessions. Be patient with your body and with yourself. Given time, you'll be amazed at what you can do and be.

Talk to your doctor or health-care professional before starting this or any other exercise program. If you have any special health conditions or concerns, consult with your health-care professional regularly to modify the exercises to work for you.

TOOLS OF THE TRADE: What you need

You can do yoga almost anywhere. You don't need much more than your body and a small patch of level ground. You can practice yoga indoors or outdoors — the key is to find someplace spacious, calm and quiet.

Indoors, your space should be clean and clutter-free — you don't want to be bumping into furniture. Aim for good airflow without it being cold or drafty. Always practice on the floor. Use a blanket or yoga mat, but avoid thick exercise mats or mattresses because they won't give your body the support it needs. You're guaranteed to fall over if you try to balance on one foot on a spongy surface.

Outside, find somewhere beautiful with level ground so you can enjoy nature around you, but stay out of the wind and direct sunlight so you don't catch cold or get sunburned. Look out for distractions — a soccer ball to the head would disturb the concentration of even the most accomplished yogini!

What to Wear

Keep it simple — wear comfortable clothes you can move in, like a tank top and shorts or a T-shirt and leggings. Natural fabrics like cotton are best because they breathe.

Loose-fitting clothes are great, but avoid things that are too baggy. You don't want your T-shirt falling in your face when you bend forward to touch your toes.

Your muscles can tense up and get stiff if they get cold, so keep a sweatshirt or sweater handy to put on for relaxation poses. Your body cools down super fast once you stop moving.

YOGA PROPS

Yoga props are things that can help make the poses easier, depending on your strength and flexibility. They aren't essential, but they are popular and are used in a few of the poses, so here's a detailed list.

⊙ Yoga (sticky) mat

This is exactly what it sounds like — a rubber mat that's kind of sticky so you won't slip and hurt yourself. When you're working so hard that sweat is dripping off the end of your nose, you can bet it's dripping off everything else, too. Let's just say you'll be happy for the non-slip surface. The yoga mat is probably the most important of all the props because it gives you cushioning and keeps you from getting dirty if you're outside. And it won't slip around like a blanket might. You can buy a mat at most fitness stores or online.

⊙ Blanket

A blanket has a few uses in your yogic practice. You can cover up with it during relaxation or meditation poses so you don't get cold. You can also fold it or roll it up to support your body in different positions. Make sure your blanket is thick wool or cotton. Synthetic or loosely woven blankets are too slippery and squishy.

⊙ Bolster

Bolsters are firm, cylindrical or rectangular pillows. They're used to support your body in different poses, especially during the relaxation poses. But don't worry if you don't have one — you can always use a folded or rolled blanket instead.

⊙ Yoga strap or belt

This is a tool to help you reach parts of your body that might seem too far away at first. You can buy an adjustable strap made of soft cotton fabric, but any long cloth belt will do. If your belt has a buckle, make sure it doesn't get in your way.

⊙ Yoga blocks

These are designed to give you a solid support to press against when you can't quite reach the floor. They are usually made of wood or very firm foam. If you find you need a block, you can also try taping together two or three hardcover books for a homemade version. (Just make sure to use books nobody wants anymore!)

GETTING STARTED:
A beginner's yoga sequence

If you're new to yoga, you might not know that *asana* is the Sanskrit word for a pose that directs your body's energy. By following particular movements, you work your body into a full asana. Different poses give different parts of your body a deep stretch, which is why asanas are done in a specific sequence.

As a beginner, it's easier to move in and out of the poses instead of holding yourself in the deep stretches. That's why most of the poses in this section are dynamic asanas, which means you're always in motion and moving in time with your breath. Sound confusing? Don't stress! Follow the instructions for breathing, and before long, timing your body's movements to the breaths you're taking will be second nature.

Even simple poses can be challenging to the most advanced yogini. The key is to practice yoga with awareness. Yoga isn't just about following the steps — if you start thinking about the phone calls you want to make or topics for your next project, you've missed the point. Take the time to really feel what the poses are doing. While you're moving, do a Q&A. Do you feel warm or cool? Can you feel any tingles? What's going on with your breathing? Your mood? Are you calm, anxious, happy or sad? Checking in by asking yourself these kinds of questions will help build your mind–body connection.

The calm, settled feeling you'll have at the end of this series sets you up perfectly for pranayama, or breath practice. Try the beginner techniques (page 62) for 5 minutes or more and then one of the meditations (page 66). They are much easier just after practicing yoga.

Above all, have fun! Yoga is one of the best ways to get to know your body and who you are. Follow the instructions and use the illustrations as a guide. Listen to your body and respect what it's telling you. Pain and discomfort mean stop and adjust. If you can't feel a thing, try to stretch a little deeper. The full pose can take a while to master, so enjoy exactly where you are — every day is a new day.

Rowing the boat pose
— NAUKA SANCHALASANA

WHY DO IT?

This pose works on the abdomen by massaging your organs (stomach, colon, liver, spleen, etc.), and strengthens the muscles that help support your spine. It warms you up and teaches you how to move with your breath.

HOW TO

STEP 1: Sit with your legs stretched out straight in front of you, knees and ankles touching. Your back should be straight, with the top of your head reaching up toward the sky, your shoulders relaxed and your arms at your sides.

STEP 2: Picture yourself sitting in a rowboat ready to row. Extend your arms and clasp imaginary oars with your hands.

STEP 3: As you breathe in, lean back as far as you can and feel your abdominal muscles start to work. At the same time, draw your hands up your body past your armpits to reach them over your head.

STEP 5: Breathe in and draw your hands up the sides of your legs to come back to a sitting position. Continue breathing in as you lean back again, ready to repeat rowing.

This is one round. Continue this circular rowing motion, moving in time with your breath. Row like this 9 more times and then reverse the movement 10 times, as if you are rowing backward.

SOMETHING DIFFERENT

To feel a different stretch in your legs, try separating your legs into a V shape. Keep your legs straight. Row over your right leg first, then your left and then between your legs. Repeat 10 times. Then try each movement backward 10 times.

STEP 4: As you breathe out, bend forward at the hips and reach your hands to the outsides of your feet.

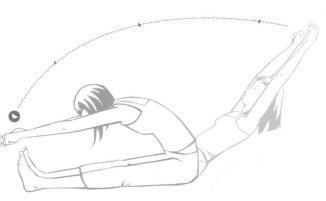

Cat pose — MARJARIASANA

WHY DO IT?

Pretending to be a cat is an easy way to loosen up the spine. This stretch tones the spinal nerves, which can help your internal organs work better. This is also a good pose for relieving menstrual cramps.

HOW TO

STEP 1: On your hands and knees, make a table with your body. Your hands should be directly under your shoulders, fingers pointing forward. Make sure your thighs are at a right angle to the floor and your back is straight. This is called a neutral position because you are not stretching in any direction.

STEP 2: As you breathe in, tilt your tailbone up, relax your belly to curve your spine down toward the ground and lift your chin, looking up to the sky. Fill your lungs completely.

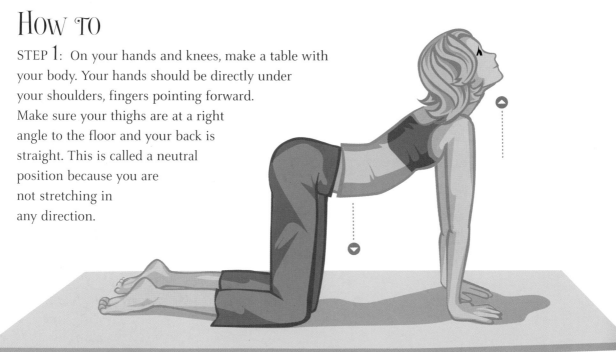

STEP 3: As you breathe out, tuck your tailbone toward the floor, curve your spine up to the sky and tuck your chin to your chest until your head is between your arms and you can see your thighs. Pull your belly button up toward your spine, completely emptying your lungs.

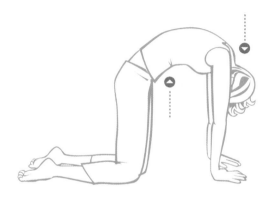

This is one round. Repeat 10 or more times, moving smoothly from one stretch to the other with your breath, just like a stretching cat. To come out of the pose, return to neutral with a straight spine and sit back onto your heels, with the tops of your feet flat on your mat.

FEELING MORE LIKE A TIGER?

Once you've got the smooth motion of the spine happening, add leg movement for even more stretch. Starting with the right leg, breathe in, reaching your knee to your nose.

Then quickly kick your leg back as you breathe out, reaching your toes up and over toward your head. A controlled kick is more important than speed here. Do five rounds with your right leg and five rounds with your left.

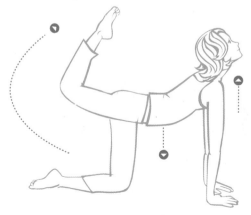

19

Swaying palm tree pose

— TIRYAKA TADASANA

WHY DO IT?

This pose is great for stretching the sides of the waist. Like Rowing the Boat pose (page 16), it works on the abdominal muscles and stretches the spine. Practicing this pose will help you develop balance, which helps to calm your mind.

HOW TO

STEP 1: Stand up straight with your feet hipbone-width apart. Focus on a point in front of you.

STEP 2: As you breathe in, reach your arms above your head with your fingers entwined and your palms turned up to the sky. Relax your shoulders.

STEP 3: As you breathe out, bend to the right, keeping your body in a straight line.

STEP 4: Hold this briefly at a full stretch, pushing your left foot down into the floor and your left hip out to the side. Keep reaching up and over with your arms.

STEP 5: As you breathe in, straighten up, keeping your arms and chest lifted.

STEP 6: As you breathe out, bend to the left, pushing the right foot down into the floor and your right hip out to the side.

STEP 7: Breathe in to come back to the center.

This is one round. Repeat 10 times. Once back to the center, breathe out as you lower your arms to your sides.

Helpful hint

Pretend your body is sandwiched between two panes of glass, one in front of you and one behind. It doesn't matter how far over to the side you bend as long as your body stays flat between the glass. If you're not sure, have a friend look at you from the side to check that your body is in line.

Too easy?

For more of a challenge, try this asana while standing on the balls of your feet.

21

Lying full spinal twist
— SHAVA UDARAKARSHANASANA

WHY DO IT?

This full spinal twist helps get rid of any tightness in your back and recharges your energy. Breathing deeply in this pose gives your abdominal organs a nice massage, too.

HOW TO

STEP 1: Lie on your back with your arms stretched out to the sides and your palms flat on the floor.

STEP 2: Bend your right leg so your foot is flat on the floor, close to your bum.

STEP 3: Pressing your foot into the floor, lift your hips up and shift them over about 10 cm (4 in.) to the right.

STEP 4: Breathe in. As you breathe out, slowly lower your knee to the left and roll onto the side of your left hip.

STEP 5: Breathe in. As you breathe out, turn your head to the right to look at your hand. This is the full spinal twist. Stay in this position for 10 deep, relaxed breaths.

STEP 6: Breathe in, bringing your head and knee back to the center. Press your right foot back into the floor, then lift your hips and shift them back to the center.

STEP 7: As you breathe out, straighten your leg.

This is one round. Repeat on your other side.

Tree pose — EKA PADA PRANAMASANA

WHY DO IT?

When you're stressed out, it's hard to concentrate and you can become clumsy, which makes you feel even worse. Tree pose is perfect for those times. Developing balance helps to calm your mind. This pose also strengthens your feet, ankles and legs and lengthens your spine. Try not to be afraid of falling over when you're in the full pose. After all, trees often sway — it's part of the game.

HOW TO

STEP 1: Stand up straight with your feet together. Focus on making your breathing relaxed and steady. Press into the ground with your feet and reach up to the sky with the top of your head. Fix your gaze on an eye-level spot that won't move, even if you do.

STEP 2: Shift your weight onto your right foot and tighten the muscles of your entire right leg, without locking your knee.

STEP 3: Place your left foot on the inside of your right thigh, toes pointing down and knee pointing out to the side. Keep your hipbones level and facing forward.

STEP 4: Bring your hands to your heart in prayer position (palms and fingers pressed together with fingers pointing up) and steady yourself.

STEP 5: When you're ready, breathe in, stretching your arms up. This is the full pose. Hold this position for up to nine breaths.

STEP 6: Reverse out of the pose gracefully, lowering your hands to your heart and then your foot to the ground.

Try to feel yourself as the connection between the earth and the sky. Switch legs and practice on the other side for the same number of breaths.

THE RIGHT CONNECTION ...

Your foot may not reach your upper thigh when you're first getting started. No worries — place it anywhere on the inside of your leg except pressing into your knee, which isn't good for your knee joint.

Downward facing dog
— ADHO MUKHA SAVASANA

WHY DO IT?

This active relaxation pose (your body's really working but you still feel pretty chilled out) strengthens the muscles in your arms and legs. It also tones the upper part of your spine between your shoulder blades. Because it's an inversion, a pose where your hips are higher than your head, your brain and face get a fresh blood supply, which helps energize you. Done regularly, Downward facing dog can help clear up pimply skin, but make sure to skip this pose when you have your period.

HOW TO

STEP 1: Start in the neutral Cat pose (page 18, step 1). As you breathe in, turn your toes under, and as you breathe out, push into the floor with your hands and feet. Straighten your legs and lift your bum up to the sky.

STEP 2: Breathing smoothly, shift your weight back and forth until you're pressing into the floor equally with your hands and feet.

STEP 3: Try to touch your heels to the ground if they don't already. Don't stress if they don't — they'll get there eventually.

STEP 4: Tuck in your chin slightly so you can see your feet. Relax the space between your shoulder blades and straighten your spine.

STEP 5: Try to slow down your breathing and feel fully supported by the ground. This is the full pose. Take nine long, slow breaths.

STEP 6: To come out of the pose, slowly lower your knees back to the floor, sit back on your heels, with the tops of your feet flat on the mat, and relax your arms.

This is one round. Repeat one to three times.

Is your back really straight?

To make sure your back is straight in the full pose, bend slightly at your knees. Stretch so the top of your head is reaching for your fingers and your tailbone is reaching for the sky. Do you feel your spine grow longer? See if you can keep that feeling while you straighten your legs.

Feeling frisky?

Move smoothly from Downward facing dog into Upward facing dog, keeping your hands and feet in place. As you breathe in, lower your hips toward the ground. Arch your back and push your chest forward and up. Look up to the sky. Move between positions five times, breathing in to get into Upward facing dog and breathing out to get into Downward facing dog.

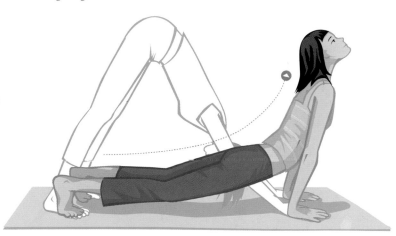

Thunderbolt pose —VAJRASANA

WHY DO IT?

This is the easiest of all the sitting poses because you don't have to work at keeping your back straight. It's very calming and great for your digestion. It's also perfect if you're suffering from a painful period.

HOW TO

STEP 1: Start on your hands and knees, with your knees together and your big toes touching.

STEP 2: Slowly sit back, placing your bum in the little cradle your feet have made. Your heels should be on either side of your hips.

STEP 3: Place your hands on your thighs and relax your whole body.

This is the full pose. Close your eyes and concentrate on your breathing. Start by holding this position for nine breaths.

STEP 4: To come out of the pose, lean forward, put your weight on your hands and stretch your legs out behind you one at a time.

IF IT HURTS

⊙ If your feet cramp, come out of the pose. Sit on your bum, grab your ankles and shake your feet gently until the cramps are gone. Once you're comfy, go back and try the full pose again.

⊙ If the pain is in your ankles or knees, try placing a rolled-up blanket or bolster under your bum. This will take some of the pressure off your ankles and knees.

⊙ If your thighs are hurting, separate your knees a bit.

Corpse pose — SAVASANA

WHY DO IT?

This relaxation pose teaches you how to calm your whole body just by using your mind. It takes practice, and even though pretending to be dead sounds creepy, you'll be amazed at how refreshed you feel when you're finished. You can do Corpse pose before starting, in between or after your poses to check in with your body or whenever you feel physically or mentally tired.

HOW TO

STEP 1: Lie on your back with your legs hipbone-width apart. Place your arms at your sides without touching your body, palms up. Your hips, chest, shoulders and head should be in line. Tuck something flat and soft under your head if you need to. If you feel cool, cover yourself with a blanket.

STEP 2: Close your eyes and feel all the places where your body is touching the floor. Start at the back of your head and work all the way down to your heels.

STEP 3: Try to feel your body become so heavy that it could sink into the floor, and if you tried to get up, it would be almost impossible.

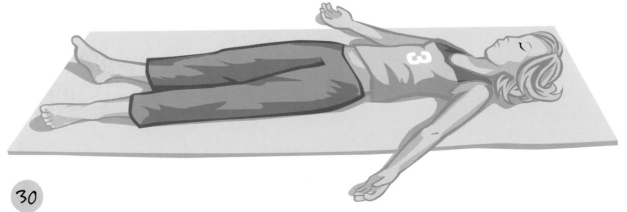

STEP 4: See the darkness behind your eyelids. Feel that darkness through your whole body and around you, empty and peaceful.

STEP 5: Become aware of your breath. Breathing through your nose, feel your breath come into your body, your abdomen rise and then your chest expand. Feel your breath leave your body in exactly the reverse direction. Start counting backward with each breath like this: "Breathe in 27, breathe out 27; breathe in 26, breathe out 26 ..." If you lose your count, just start again. Continue as long as you have time to practice and try not to fall asleep.

STEP 6: When you are ready to come out of the pose, keep your eyes closed and slowly begin moving your fingers and toes, gently waking up your body.

STEP 7: Bring your knees to your chest and roll over onto your right side, curled up like a baby. Slowly sit up. Sit for a moment and feel your completely relaxed body. Open your eyes slowly. Don't stand up too suddenly or you might get a little dizzy.

CAN'T RELAX?

If you can feel at the beginning that your body is holding onto tension, try tensing up your body while lying on the floor. Clench everything and hold your breath. Then breathe out, releasing all your tension, and relax back onto the floor. Try this with your whole body or work your way around your body, part by part — whatever works best for you.

GOING FURTHER:
A more advanced yoga sequence

Once you've been doing all the beginner asanas with the suggested number of repetitions regularly for at least a month, you'll be ready for something new.

Now you'll be holding each full pose longer instead of moving in and out of it quickly. These poses are all about stamina, concentration and strength.

It's hard work, but if you feel any pain or discomfort, come out of the pose, relax and try again. With practice, it gets easier and you'll be able to stay in the poses longer without clock-watching.

The stillness in these more advanced poses works on your body in a different way from the movements of the beginner sequence. By now you've learned to move your body with your breath. Now see what your breath can do for you while you're holding a pose.

For example, if you're breathing out while you're bending forward, try to control the movement so you reach your full stretch at the same time as you empty your lungs.

In the pose, use your in-breath as a mini pit stop to relax and feel the effects. With your next breath out, stretch a little further into the pose if you can.

Whatever you do, keep breathing — it'll feel like less of a struggle if you focus on that.

If you want a longer practice, sprinkle in some of the poses you already know. A relaxation pose like Corpse (page 30) at the very end of your practice can be way more satisfying than going to the kitchen for a piece of chocolate cake! You can now start to spend more time doing pranayama and meditation. Build up gradually — enlightenment isn't going anywhere.

Forward bend pose
— PASCHIMOTTANASANA

WHY DO IT?

This pose is one of the most powerful forward bends for the spine. When your spine is healthy, the positive effects trickle through your whole body. This pose also loosens your hip joints and gives your hamstrings a deep stretch. This is great to practice just before meditation, especially if you don't have time to do a full yoga session.

HOW TO

STEP 1: Sit with your legs straight in front of you, your back straight and your hands in prayer position (page 24) over your heart. Your heels should be pushing away from you and the backs of your knees touching the floor so your legs are working. Relax your back muscles.

STEP 2: As you breathe in, lift your hands over your head, stretching up.

STEP 3: As you breathe out, slowly bend forward at your hips, keeping your back straight and your arms stretched out. Bend as far forward as you can, still keeping your legs and back straight.

STEP 4: Grab on to your big toes with your thumbs and index fingers. If they're out of reach, hold your ankles or calves or use a yoga strap around your feet.

STEP 5: As you breathe in, feel where you're tight and try to relax those muscles. As you breathe out, use your abdominal muscles and arms to pull yourself farther down and forward. You'll feel an amazing stretch up the back of your legs and all the way up your spine. This is the full pose. Close your eyes and breathe deeply.

STEP 6: To come out, breathe out and straighten your arms out in front of you. Breathe in as you slowly return to the starting position with your back straight and your hands in prayer position. Breathe out, bringing your arms down to your sides.

At first, try holding the full pose for three long breaths. Work up to holding the pose for 2 to 5 minutes. Repeat one to three times.

DON'T OVERDO IT!

Relaxing in a deep stretch like this takes practice. It might feel uncomfortable until you get used to it, but if you feel any sharp pains, you're pushing too hard.

Cobra pose — BHUJANGASANA

WHY DO IT?

Cobra pose bends the spine in the opposite direction of Forward bend pose, continuing to tone the spinal nerves and keep your spine flexible. The healthier your spinal nerves are, the better your brain communicates with the rest of your body.

HOW TO

STEP 1: Lie on your stomach with your chin tucked in so your forehead is flat on the floor. Your legs should be together and your toes pointing straight behind you.

STEP 2: Bend your arms and place your palms on the floor beside your shoulders. Line up your fingertips with your shoulders, pointing your fingers forward. Your elbows will stick up, but keep them close to your body.

STEP 3: Press your legs and feet into the floor and feel the ground as you prepare to lift your head.

STEP 4: As you breathe in, relax your shoulders and start drawing your nose and then your chin along the floor away from your body to lift your head up to the sky. Continue looking up until the curling movement reaches into your upper back.

STEP 5: Peel your upper body off the floor using your abdominal and spinal muscles, keeping your hands relaxed and your elbows close to your body. Feel your chest moving up and forward. This is the full pose. Look up at the sky. Hold for three to five breaths.

STEP 6: Breathing out, slowly reverse the movements to come out of the pose.

Repeat up to five times, relaxing on your belly and breathing deeply for three or more breaths between each repetition.

BELLY FLOP RELAXATION

To relax completely between repetitions, turn your head to the side, resting on your ear. Bring your arms down to your sides, palms up, leaving some space between them and your body. Turn your feet in so that your big toes touch. Rest here, feeling your whole body melt into the floor. Alternate the side you turn your head to each time.

Triangle pose — TRIKONASANA

WHY DO IT?

This side stretch is great for revitalizing your whole body. It energizes and stretches your leg and back muscles, tones your waist and improves your appetite. Feeling nervous or depressed? Try this pose to help wash those feelings away.

HOW TO

STEP 1: Stand with your feet one leg-length apart. Lift your arms out to the sides at shoulder height, palms down. Keeping your heels in place, turn your right foot all the way out and your left foot in slightly.

STEP 2: Take a deep breath in, and as you breathe out, reach out with your right hand to bend sideways. You can bend your right knee slightly if you need to, but keep your upper body from bending forward. Picture your body sandwiched between two panes of glass.

STEP 3: Bend sideways until your left hand points up to the sky. Turn your head to look up toward your hand and keep your left heel firmly on the floor. This is the full pose.

STEP 4: You can take the full pose further by turning your head to look forward and slowly reaching your left arm over until it touches your left ear. Feel the stretch down the left side of your body all the way to your heel. Take up to nine breaths in whichever full pose you choose.

I'M NO TRIANGLE!

If reaching your toes or the floor is absolutely out of the question, grab a yoga block and place it right beside your right foot. Press into the block and lift your hips to keep your left foot planted on the floor to give you the support you need.

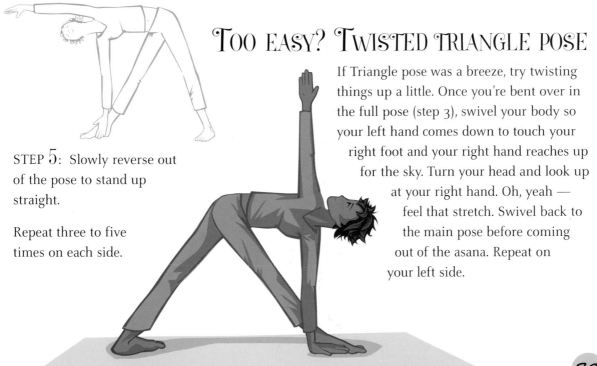

STEP 5: Slowly reverse out of the pose to stand up straight.

Repeat three to five times on each side.

TOO EASY? TWISTED TRIANGLE POSE

If Triangle pose was a breeze, try twisting things up a little. Once you're bent over in the full pose (step 3), swivel your body so your left hand comes down to touch your right foot and your right hand reaches up for the sky. Turn your head and look up at your right hand. Oh, yeah — feel that stretch. Swivel back to the main pose before coming out of the asana. Repeat on your left side.

Twisting squat pose
— PAVRITI UTKATASANA

WHY DO IT?

This is one of the best poses for heating up your body. The deep squat with the legs squeezed together is ideal for strengthening your legs. In Sanskrit, utkatasana means "fierce pose," and with practice you'll become more powerful and ready to take action.

HOW TO

STEP 1: Stand with your feet together and your hips, chest, shoulders and head all in a straight line.

STEP 2: As you breathe in, lift up your arms, fingers reaching to the sky. Relax your shoulders.

STEP 3: As you breathe out, squat down, squeezing your thighs and knees together.

STEP 4: Lean forward a little to balance yourself, and tuck your pelvis under to straighten and protect your lower back. At the same time, lift your chest, arching your upper back slightly.

STEP 5: Look up to your hands and breathe deeply for several breaths, feeling the power and heat rise from your legs through your body.

STEP 6: Staying in the squat, lower your hands to prayer position at your heart (page 24). As you breathe in, twist your whole upper body to the right.

STEP 7: Breathe out as you slowly slide your left hand down the outside of your right thigh and place your palm on the floor beside your right foot. Breathe in and lift your right arm straight to the sky as you twist your chest to the side. Turn your head to look toward your right hand.

STEP 8: Keep squeezing your legs together and pull your belly button back to your spine. This is the full pose. After three relaxed breaths, return your hands to the prayer position and repeat the twist on the opposite side for three breaths.

STEP 9: To come out of the pose, return your hands to prayer position and come back to the center. As you breathe in, slowly stand up. Take three deep breaths.

Repeat three times. Work up to holding the twist for nine breaths on each side.

Warrior pose — VIRA BHADRASANA

Why do it?

This pose builds strength, especially in your leg muscles. Your open chest and feeling of stability on your feet will help you feel your inner strength. Because it takes some balance, this asana will also build your concentration. This pose has many variations, so if you try a few yoga classes you're guaranteed to learn other ways to do it, too.

How to

STEP 1: Stand up straight with your feet together and your arms at your sides.

STEP 2: As you breathe in, step your right foot out wide to the side while you lift your arms out to shoulder height, palms down, over your feet. Turn your right foot out and turn your left foot slightly in.

STEP 3: As you breathe out, use your thigh muscles to keep your feet pressing into the floor and your knees from rolling inward.

STEP 4: Take a deep breath in, and as you breathe out, bend your right knee until your right thigh is parallel to the floor. Check to make sure your knee is directly over your ankle.

STEP 5: Turn your head to look to your right hand and breathe deeply. This is the full pose.

STEP 6: To come out of the pose, turn your head and feet back to center. Then step your feet back together, lowering your arms to your sides.

Build up to taking nine breaths in the full pose. Repeat up to three times on each side.

Staying Strong

⊙ Reach out with your middle fingertips to keep your shoulders even and your chest open.

⊙ Keep your hipbones level and facing forward.

⊙ You should almost feel like you are leaning back over your back leg to keep your torso upright over your hips.

⊙ Really ground yourself by pushing into the floor with the outside of your back foot.

Balancing stick pose

— EKA PADASANA

WHY DO IT?

This pose takes a combo of strength and balance, and looks easier than it is. The balancing element works on your concentration, while the strength element tones your legs, hips, arms and wrists. The full body stretch releases tension in your lower back.

HOW TO

STEP 1: Stand up straight with your feet together and your arms at your sides.

STEP 2: Breathe in and lift your arms overhead, clasping your hands together, index fingers pointing to the sky.

STEP 3: Step forward with your right foot and plant it solidly on the floor with your toes pointing forward and your leg straight.

STEP 4: As you breathe out, begin bending forward slowly while you lift your left leg straight out behind you and reach your arms out in front of you.

STEP 5: Continue bending forward until your arms, body and left leg form a straight line. This is the full pose. Take relaxed, natural breaths and stay in the pose as long as you can without straining.

STEP 6: To come out of the pose, breathe in while you slowly lift your torso upright and lower your left leg back to the floor. Once you are standing on both feet, release your hands and breathe out, lowering your arms to your sides.

Repeat up to three times on each side.

44

Staying Balanced

⊙ Keep your standing-leg muscles pulling up and your hipbones level with the floor, without locking your knee.

⊙ Fix your gaze on a point on the floor about 1 m (3 ft.) in front of you.

⊙ Reach your fingers and pointed toes away from each other.

⊙ Get a friend to make sure your body isn't curving to the side like a banana.

Too difficult?

Bend only as far forward as you can without falling over. As you practice and get stronger, gradually bend farther forward.

Dancer pose
— NATARAJASANA

WHY DO IT?

The Dancer is a beautiful and graceful balancing pose
that also develops your concentration skills. Your
standing leg is toned while the held leg is stretched.
Your chest is opened, which improves your lung
capacity, and as an added bonus, you get a back bend.

HOW TO

STEP 1: Stand up straight with your feet together
and your arms at your sides. Lift your right arm
out to the side, palm up.

STEP 2: Shift your weight completely onto
your left foot and bend your right leg to
bring your foot up to your bum. Your knees
should stay together. Reach behind you with
your right hand and grab around the inside
of your ankle with a firm grip.

STEP 3: Breathe in and lift your left arm up to the sky.

STEP 4: Breathing out slowly, push your foot out and up into your right hand.

STEP 6: To come out, straighten your body and release your foot, coming out of the pose as gracefully as you went in. (Letting your leg crash down to the floor is not graceful.)

Take three relaxing breaths standing in the starting position. Repeat one to three times on each side.

STEP 5: As you push out with your foot, begin bending your body forward, looking at your left hand, which has your index finger and thumb together in Gyana mudra (page 65). This is the full pose. Hold for up to nine breaths.

STAYING STEADY

◉ Ground yourself on your left foot by making all the muscles in your leg work.

◉ Try to stretch equally in opposite directions from your toes to your fingers.

◉ Keep your hipbones level, even if you don't go as far into the pose.

Locust pose — SHALABHASANA

WHY DO IT?

The Locust is a whole lot more than just a back bend. In this pose you use your lower back muscles, strengthening an area we tend to ignore. Your whole abdominal area gets a deep massage, helping your stomach and bowels work like a well-oiled machine.

HOW TO

STEP 1: Lie on your stomach with your neck stretched long and your chin resting on the floor. Your legs should be together, with the tops of your feet on your mat. Place your arms at your sides, palms down. Or tuck your arms underneath your body so your elbows are close together and your hands, palms down, are under your upper thighs.

STEP 2: Breathe out all the air from your lungs and then breathe in deeply. Keeping your chin, shoulders and hips on the floor, raise your left leg slowly. Hold your leg up for a few seconds, reaching away from you with your toes. Slowly lower your leg and then breathe out completely.

STEP 3: Breathe in deeply and repeat the sequence, lifting your right leg.

STEP 4: Tucking in your chin and pressing your lips into the floor, breathe in deeply again and this time lift both legs. Keep your legs straight and together. This takes a lot of effort, so hold for a shorter time and then slowly lower your legs before breathing out.

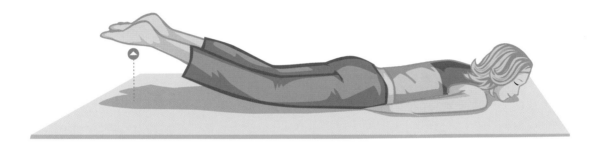

STEP 5: Turn your head to the side and relax your body completely in a belly flop, as you did after Cobra pose (page 36). Let your breathing return to its natural rhythm.

Repeat the whole set three to five times.

Bridge pose — SETU BANDHASANA

WHY DO IT?

The Bridge is an inversion pose that prepares you for more advanced inversions you might try with a yoga teacher. Your legs get a workout while your pelvic area, abdomen, shoulders and back get a great stretch. At the same time, your brain gets a fresh surge of blood, which boosts your brainpower and calms you down. Feeling chilled out while energized and alert is a beautiful thing. And remember, since this is an inversion pose, skip it while you have your period.

HOW TO

STEP 1: Lie on your back and place your heels on the floor close to your bum so your toes point in a little in and your knees point up. Grab your ankles.

STEP 2: Breathe in. As you breathe out, press your feet and arms into the floor as you lift your pelvis up to the sky and your chest toward your chin.

STEP 3: Relax your breathing and make sure your knees are pulling toward each other, your neck is relaxed and your back is strong in the arch. It's very important to keep your head straight and your chin tucked. This is the full pose. Close your eyes and focus on taking nine slow, relaxed breaths from your abdomen.

STEP 4: To come out, breathe out as you slowly lower your bum back to the floor. Pull your knees in to your chest and rock gently from side to side to release any tension in your back.

Repeat one to three times. Work up to holding the pose for 2 to 5 minutes.

IT'S ALL ABOUT HEART

Instead of grabbing your ankles, try
entwining your fingers and rolling your
shoulders open to bring your shoulder
blades together once you have lifted
your pelvis. This lifts your chest a little
higher and opens it to the sky. Breathe
deeply and feel the openness
around your heart. To come
out, release your hands
and reverse out as usual.

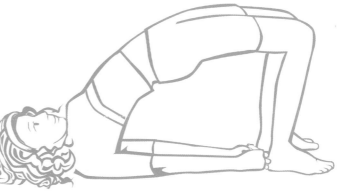

Lion pose — SIMHASANA

WHY DO IT?

Whether you are an aspiring rock star, in a public speaking contest or just want to avoid getting a sore throat, this pose is for you. It works to develop your voice and confidence. It improves circulation to the tongue and throat. It stimulates your eyes and releases tension in your chest and diaphragm (the muscle that helps you fill and empty your lungs). You might feel a little silly growling like a wild animal at first, but it's worth it.

HOW TO

STEP 1: If you can, face the sun and sit in Thunderbolt pose (page 28) with your knees about 45 cm (18 in.) apart.

STEP 2: Place your hands on the floor between your knees, palms down and fingers pointing toward you. Your arms should be straight.

STEP 3: Lean forward onto your hands. Spread your fingers and tense up your whole body.

STEP 4: Tilt your head to look up toward the sky.

STEP 5: Breathe in through your nose and push your chest forward through your arms, arching your back.

STEP 6: Open your mouth wide and stick your tongue out as far as you can.

STEP 7: As you breathe out, make a slow and steady "ahhhh" sound. Feel the vibrations travel through your body.

STEP 8: Close your mouth, relax your whole body and return to Thunderbolt pose. Close your eyes and take a deep breath. This is one round.

Repeat three to five times.

Too difficult?

If your legs are uncomfortable, place a folded blanket or bolster between your heels and bum. Place your hands on your knees if you can't touch the floor. Follow the rest of the pose as usual.

Too easy?
Playful lion

For more stretch, add to this posture by stretching one leg out behind you. Bend that leg and point your toes up to the sky. This is the lion's tail. Move your foot from left to right to wag the tail, stretching your hip muscles and the front of your leg. Do this for each leg.

Vocal lion

While breathing out and growling, move your tongue slowly from side to side. As the sound changes, feel the added stretch in your tongue and throat.

53

Lotus pose — PADMASANA

WHY DO IT?

This is the most famous of all the yoga asanas. It's the perfect pose for keeping the body still and the mind calm. With practice you can sit perfectly still for long periods of time — perfect for pranayama and meditation (pages 62 and 66). However, this pose shouldn't be forced and isn't good for people with weak or sore knees.

HOW TO

STEP 1: Sit on the floor with your legs in front of you. Bend one leg and place your foot on the upper thigh of your other leg so the sole of the foot faces up.

STEP 2: Try to relax and get comfortable in your position. Then bend your straight leg and place your foot on top of your other leg so your shins cross. Ideally, your knees touch the floor. (Don't worry — that might take a while.)

STEP 3: Place your hands on your knees in Gyana or Chin mudra (page 65). Straighten your back and neck and relax your shoulders.

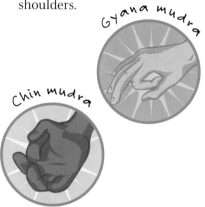

Gyana mudra

Chin mudra

STEP 4: Close your eyes and try to sit quietly and still for as long as you feel comfortable. With each practice, try to hold this pose longer.

Next time you practice, switch which leg goes on top.

PRETZEL LEGS

To make Lotus pose easier, try sitting on a cushion or folded blanket to lift your hips. Or try Butterfly pose, Titaliasana, to build up the flexibility in your hips. Sitting up, place your heels together and draw them close to your groin, holding them in place with your hands. With your back straight, flap your knees up and down like a butterfly.

Lotus pose with cushion

Butterfly pose

ALMOST THERE

If the Full lotus is just out of reach, try the Half lotus, where only one foot is on top and the other is tucked in beside your inner thigh. It doesn't look that different, but you'll be surprised how much easier it is.

YOGA PLUS:
Getting even more out of your practice

This may come as a bit of a surprise, but there's a lot more to yoga than the poses. This section will introduce you to a few more ways you can add to your practice — and your fun.

One way of practicing Hatha yoga is by doing something called vinyasa, or a yogic flow. A vinyasa is a series of asanas that are strung together, and you move from one pose to the next in time with each breath.

Pranayama, or breath practice, is the yogini's secret weapon that can be practiced anytime, anywhere.

Little add-ons like the mudras, or simple hand gestures, or the chanting of mantras like that famous "OM" are small ways you can make your poses even more powerful.

And if you're not sure how to find your chakras or even what a chakra is, just keep reading.

Last but not least, meditation, in its own quiet way, is going to rock your world. It's different for everyone, but many people who meditate regularly believe that it's changed their life in some way.

Vinyasa

Why do it?

The Sun salutation, or Surya namaskara, is a vinyasa that is considered a new addition to yoga even though it's been around for a while. It's a great practice because it works your whole body, inside and out. Whether you need revving up or calming down, you can use it to find the balance you are looking for. You can practice the Sun salutation anytime, but the best times are at sunrise and sunset. It's also a great warm-up before the other poses.

Making a connection between your movements and your breath is very important in this practice. Learn the sequence and then try to flow through it, moving from one pose to the next in time with your breathing.

Many variations of the Sun salutation are found in different yoga classes and traditions. Here's a basic one to get you started.

How to

STEP 1: Prayer pose (Pranamasana) — Stand up straight, hands in prayer position (page 24) over your heart. Relax your body and breathe calmly.

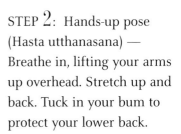

STEP 2: Hands-up pose (Hasta utthanasana) — Breathe in, lifting your arms up overhead. Stretch up and back. Tuck in your bum to protect your lower back.

STEP 3: Hand-to-foot pose (Padahastasana) — Breathe out, bending forward. Place your hands on either side of your feet (or on your calves or ankles if you can't quite reach). Tuck in your chin and try to keep your legs straight.

STEP 4: Lunge pose (Ashwa sanchalanasana) — Breathe in, stepping back with your right foot, while keeping your palms on the floor. Arch your back and look up to the sky. Keep your left knee over your ankle.

STEP 5: Mountain pose (Parvatasana) — Breathe out, stepping back with your left foot. Lift your bum up to the sky and lower your head between your arms. Keep your back straight.

STEP 6: Eight limbs pose (Ashtangasana) — Without taking a breath, lower your knees, chest and chin to the floor at the same time, kind of like doing a push-up.

STEP 7: Cobra pose (Bhujangasana) — Breathe in, arching your spine and lifting your head. Lift your chest but keep your abdomen glued to the floor.

STEP 8: Mountain pose (Parvatasana) — Breathe out, pressing your hands and feet into the floor, and lift your bum up to the sky. Lower your head between your arms and keep your back straight.

STEP 9: Lunge pose (Ashwa sanchalanasana) — Breathe in, stepping forward with your left foot, while keeping your palms on the floor. Arch your back and look up to the sky. Keep your left knee over your ankle.

STEP 10: Hand-to-foot pose (Padahastasana) — Breathe out, stepping your right foot forward to join your left, and straighten your legs into the forward bend. Place your hands beside your feet and tuck in your chin.

STEP 11: Hands-up pose (Hasta utthanasana) — Breathe in, coming up to standing with a straight back, lifting your arms up overhead. Stretch up and back. Tuck in your bum to protect your lower back.

STEP 12: Prayer pose (Pranamasana) — Breathe out, coming back to the center, returning your hands to your heart. Relax.

Repeat on your left side by stepping your left foot back in step 4 and your right foot forward in step 9.

Repeat on both sides 3 to 12 times, building up gradually.

Once you've mastered the Sun salutation, try the Moon salutation, Chandra namaskara. The moon is linked to feminine energy, so this practice is perfect for girls and is ideal to do at night, as long as your belly's empty.

After steps 4 and 9, add this step to chill yourself out: Balancing in Lunge pose, breathe out as you bring your hands to prayer position (page 24). Breathe in as you extend your hands, palms together, above your head. Arch your back and look up to your hands. Hold your breath as you lower your hands back to your heart and then to the floor, laying your palms down.

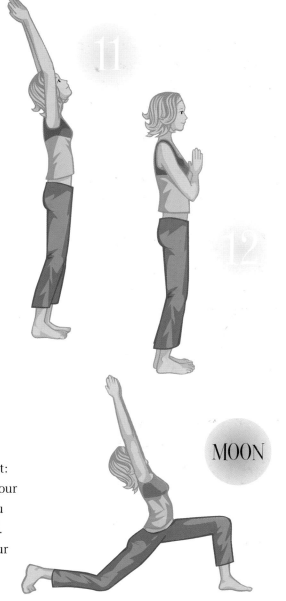

MOON

61

Pranayama

What is it?

Pranayama is often called breath control, but it's even more than that. Yogis and yoginis believe you can expand your body's life force energy, or prana, by using your breathing. They've developed special breathing techniques to cool you down, warm you up, chill you out, energize you and more. Imagine a few minutes of breathing giving you more energy than a chocolate bar — without the sugar crash. Or breathing yourself into a peaceful sleep and getting a great rest, even the night before a final exam.

Why do it?

Everyday stresses like a lack of routine, junk food binges and piles of homework are hard on your vital energy, that magic ingredient that keeps you going. Pranayama and focusing on your breathing can help you keep that energy balanced.

Here's an example of how it works. Have you ever noticed that when you're really stressed, your breathing speeds up and gets shallow? If you were to consciously take a few deep, long breaths, you would calm down. If you breathed slowly and deeply all the time, imagine how calm and focused you'd be at every moment.

Things to keep in mind

- Breathe through your nose unless other instructions are given.

- You can practice anytime, but your body will be particularly ready for pranayama after finishing your asanas.

- Do your breath work on an empty stomach.

- All that air might dry you out a little, so drink lots of water throughout the day.

- Don't do pranayama when you're sick.

- Never strain or force your breath.

- If you really get into it and want to try other variations of pranayama, find a knowledgeable teacher because you'll need some one-on-one time.

FULL YOGIC BREATH

You can practice this lying down, sitting or standing, as long as you are comfortable and relaxed. Once you get the hang of it, try breathing this way in your poses. After a while you'll be able to slow your breathing and inhale and exhale more air with each breath. But even though it's great for yoga, don't breathe like this all the time.

STEP 1: Lie on your back. Place one hand on your chest and the other on your belly.

STEP 2: Close your eyes and pay attention to the way you are breathing. Don't try to control it. Where are you breathing from? Are your breaths shallow or deep?

STEP 3: Now try breathing into your abdomen. When you breathe in, let your belly rise, and as you breathe out, let it tighten. The hand on your belly should rise and fall, while the one on your chest stays still. Do this for 27 breaths.

STEP 4: Now try breathing with your chest, which means using your rib cage to breathe in and out. Now the hand on your chest is rising and falling and the other is still. This is harder, but don't strain, and take a short pause between breaths. Do this for 27 breaths.

STEP 5: Take a breath to fill your lungs. Now try to breathe in a little more, right at the top of your lungs. Your shoulders and collarbone will lift just a tiny bit. Starting at the top of your lungs, breathe out slowly until everything including your ribs is relaxed. Do this for up to five breaths.

STEP 6: Add the breathing techniques of steps 3, 4 and 5 together and you have the full yogic breath. Start by inhaling into the abdomen, then the rib cage and finally the upper rib cage. Exhale in the reverse order. Make the breath as smooth as you can. With practice you'll be able to make it smoother and slower.

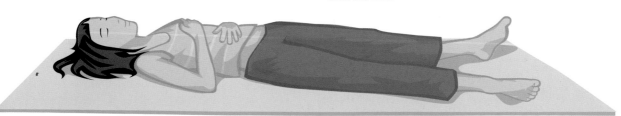

ALTERNATE NOSTRIL BREATHING

This more advanced breath is very calming and is said to balance the activity in the left and right sides of the brain. Try it if you need to clear your thoughts and concentrate.

STEP 1: Sit in a comfortable position like Thunderbolt pose (page 28) or Lotus pose (page 54).

STEP 2: Place your right index and middle fingers on your forehead, between your eyebrows. Rest your thumb on the right edge of your nose and your ring finger on the left edge.

STEP 3: Gently close off your right nostril and take five relaxed and quiet breaths in and out of the left nostril.

STEP 4: Release the right nostril and close off the left. Take five breaths on the other side.

This is one round. Practice five repetitions, slowly building up to 15 minutes. This takes time, so don't rush it. It may take weeks or months before your breath is smooth, but once your breathing is silent, you are ready for the next step.

STEP 5: Breathe in the left nostril, close it off while you open the right one and breathe out through the right. Go back and forth like this:

- Breathe in left, counting to four.
- Breathe out right, counting to four.
- Breathe in right, counting to four.
- Breathe out left, counting to four.

This is one round. Staying relaxed, start with 9 repetitions and slowly build up to practicing for 15 minutes.

Mudras

The Sanskrit word *mudra* has many different meanings. Basically, a mudra is a hand gesture that redirects the energy in your body that affects your mood or attitude. Mudras are easy ways to improve your awareness and concentration. The most famous mudra is prayer position, or Anjali mudra, with your palms together over your heart (page 24). It's used in many different cultures. Here are two other hand mudras that are perfect for making the most of your pranayama and meditation practice.

GYANA MUDRA

This is great for when you need a quiet moment and you want to connect with your sense of intuition.

STEP 1: Sit in whichever meditation pose you find the most comfortable.

STEP 2: Tuck the tips of your index fingers into the base of your thumbs. Relax the other three fingers so that they are straight and not touching each other.

STEP 3: Place the palms of your hands on your knees and relax from your shoulders all the way down to your hands.

CHIN MUDRA

This is the same as Gyana mudra but with your palms up. This works for feeling open and receptive. Try it while sitting in class to take in everything your teacher is saying. Don't get discouraged if you can't feel an effect immediately. The effect will be there even if it takes time for you to become aware of it.

Meditation

Ever notice that when you're completely into what you're doing, time seems to stand still and nothing bothers you? Unfortunately, that feeling lasts only as long as you can keep your mind focused on one thing. For most of us, our thoughts jump around like popcorn in a popper. Meditation is a way of quieting your mind. It's the ultimate chill-out and different from a daydreaming session because when you meditate, you're aware of that moment, rather than trying to escape from it using your imagination.

OUTER EYES CLOSED, INNER EYES OPEN RELAXATION

Here's a technique that's great for right after a yoga session or anytime you need to completely relax and decompress. Keep it simple or get creative — it's up to you.

⊙ Get comfortable

Lie in Corpse pose (page 30) and cover yourself with a blanket. Do a mental check-in with your body to make sure you can lie completely still for the next little while. Shift around to get comfortable if you need to.

⊙ Use your breath

Close your eyes and pay attention to your breathing. Slowly start the full yogic breath (page 63), if you can. Otherwise, just try to keep your breath deep and relaxed.

⊙ Make a promise

Think of something positive you would like to see yourself do or be. Repeat it three times from your heart, knowing that in time it will happen.

⊙ Mind over matter

Use your mind to create different sensations in your body. Feel your body become heavy and then light and floating. Feel your body go cool and then warm. Think of other opposite sensations you can try.

◉ Take a trip

Use your power of visualization to go anywhere you like. Imagine someplace you'll feel safe and relaxed and see it in your mind. Lying on a sandy beach, walking through a beautiful forest, flying through perfect white clouds ... there's no limit. Enjoy the experience even more by using your mind to create as much detail as you can — sounds, temperature, smell, etc. — but try to stay part of your visualization and not fall asleep. When you've had enough, gently come back to your physical body.

◉ Repeat your promise

Repeat your positive thought three more times. Remind yourself that when you get up you will feel completely refreshed and relaxed.

◉ Come back to your breath

Pay attention to your breath again and feel the places where your body rests on the floor.

◉ Stir

Slowly move your fingers and toes. Keep your eyes closed and gently waken your body. Turn onto your left side and draw your knees close to your chest. Come up slowly to sitting. Open your eyes slowly to get used to the light. Take this calm feeling into the rest of your day.

SITTING AND WATCHING

This is a great technique for getting rid of everyday stress. If you practice it regularly, you'll find that the things that used to get to you hardly bother you at all.

Find a quiet place, sit in your favorite meditation pose and lightly close your eyes. Try to stay still. Watch your thoughts like a TV screen. Don't judge them or try to change them. Your mind can be tricky, making you spend most of your time thinking about the past or dreaming about the future instead of being where you are right in the moment.

You might be amazed by the thoughts that come into your head. Don't worry. Over time your thoughts will quiet down when they realize they aren't getting any reaction from you.

At first try this meditation for a few minutes and, with practice, slowly increase the time. There's no rush.

Mantras

If you've been to a couple of yoga classes, you might be wondering what the deal is with "OM." The teacher might ask you to chant it at the beginning of your class and maybe at the end. There might be other unfamiliar-sounding chants, too. Welcome to the wonderful world of mantras. Mantras are words or sounds that are chanted, either out loud or in your head, to focus your mind and affect your mood and energy.

"OM" is a bija, or seed sound. The ancient yogis didn't need advanced scientific equipment to realize that everything around us, every single molecule in the universe, vibrates and creates a sound, whether you can hear it or not. They believed that the combination of all those vibrations makes the sound

"OM." By chanting this sound we can connect with the unseen movement of the universe, which means we're connecting with something far bigger than ourselves. Test it out. How does chanting "OM" with your hands in prayer position (page 24) three times at the beginning and end of your yoga session make you feel?

The effect of Sanskrit mantras can be very powerful, but you can also come up with your own mantra, or positive word or phrase. Repeating something like "I am happy, healthy and at peace in the world" a few times before and after your yoga practice can make you feel fantastic.

Chakras

Yoga works in many ways beyond giving you a tight butt. In Hatha yoga, the body is not only thought of as a skeleton with muscles on it, but also a pattern of energy moving through channels. Where the channels cross is where you find an energy center, or chakra, which means "spinning disk" in Sanskrit. The seven main chakras are located along the central channel up and down your spine.

This may sound a bit out there, but as you become comfortable with the physical part of your practice, you can add to it, if you want, by focusing on certain chakras in each pose to get a greater feeling of how the pose relates to your energy and affects your emotions. Here's a map of the main chakras to get you started. Different yoga schools have different colors for the chakras — go with what feels right for you.

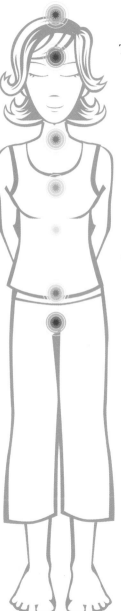

Crown chakra:
Sahasrara
clarity

Throat chakra:
Vishuddhi
communication
and creativity

**Solar Plexus
chakra:**
Manipura
power and
confidence

Root chakra:
Mooladhara
basic needs

Third Eye chakra:
Ajna
intuition

Heart chakra:
Anahata
love and
compassion

Sacral chakra:
Swadhisthana
wishes and
dreams

69

YOGA FOR ALL YOU ARE AND DO

Everyone has a favorite hobby or way of spending time. It could be sports, martial arts or dance. Or maybe reading, painting or seeing every movie that hits the theater is your thing. Whatever makes you tick, different activities call for different strengths and flexibilities. The right yoga poses can make you better and more comfortable at doing what you love to do.

An all-around yoga program like either the Getting Started (page 14) or Going Further (page 32) sequences gives you self-awareness and better concentration as well as the physical benefits. But adding specific asanas to your favorite activities as a warm-up, a cool-down or just a breather can help your performance and prevent injuries.

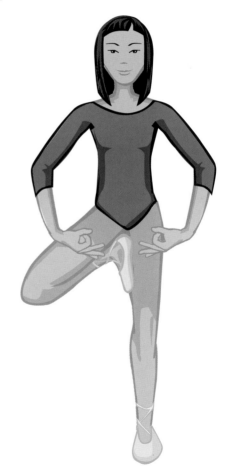

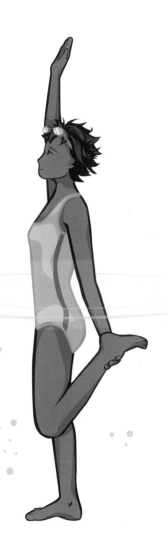

Remember that anyone can do yoga. It can be adjusted for any level of physical activity, including for those of us with physical challenges. The most important thing is to pay attention to the feedback your body is giving you. If you feel tightness or pain in a muscle, DO NOT ignore it. Explore what's causing the feeling, and think about what you can do to help it.

Take a little time to try mixing in some yoga with the other things you love. See how they can become even better. You've got nothing to lose and everything to gain.

ON YOUR MARK, GET SET, GO!

Are running sports, sprints or long-distance running your thing? Using these yoga poses regularly can help you become more aware of your body, and feeling what needs to be stretched, strengthened or rested will mean fewer injuries. And if it's speed you're after, the formula goes like this: Better flexibility = better range of motion = longer stride length = faster speed.

- ◎ Warm-up: Sun salutation (page 58)
- ◎ Calves: Downward facing dog (page 26)
- ◎ Quadriceps: Dancer pose (page 46)
- ◎ Hamstrings: Forward bend pose (page 34)
- ◎ Glutes: Tiger pose (a Cat pose variation, page 19)
- ◎ Iliotibial Band: Swaying palm tree pose (page 20)
- ◎ Hip flexors: Lunge pose from the Sun salutation (page 59)
- ◎ Spine: Lying full spinal twist (page 22)

Running sports, like soccer, rugby and field hockey, and most court sports, like basketball and volleyball, also require agility, jumping skills and extensions. This means you need to take care of your joints with special stretches. The key to doing the following exercises yogically is to concentrate on the joint and breathe with the motion.

Ankle Rotations

Sit on the ground with your legs straight. Draw circles with your toes, feeling your ankles move through their full range of motion. Draw 10 circles in each direction.

Shoulder shrugs and rotations

Stand or sit with your back straight. Breathe in, bringing your shoulders up to your ears, and then breathe out, dropping them down. Repeat 10 times. Next place your fingertips where your neck meets your shoulders so your elbows point out to the sides. Draw 10 circles forward with your elbows and then 10 backward.

Knee Rotations

Seated on the ground, bend your right leg so your thigh is close to your chest. Place your hands under your knee and relax your leg. Rotating from the knee, keep your ankle still and use your toes to draw circles. Start with small circles. Draw 10 in each direction. Repeat with your other leg.

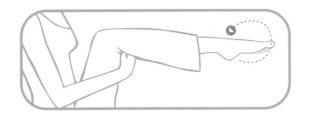

Wrist Rotations

Reach your arms out in front of you and make fists with your hands. Draw a circle with each fist, feeling your wrist joints move through their full range of motion. Draw 10 circles in each direction.

LIKE A FISH TO WATER

Swimming uses your whole body. These poses target parts of your body that will really benefit from better flexibility.

- ⊙ Warm-up: Sun salutation (page 58)
- ⊙ Shoulders: Shoulder rotations (page 73)
- ⊙ Hip flexors: Dancer pose (page 46)
- ⊙ Ankles: Ankle rotations (page 73)
- ⊙ Back: Cat pose (page 18)
- ⊙ Overall body: Moving from Upward to Downward facing dog (page 27)

If you have a favorite stroke, ask yourself which parts of your body are really being put to the test. Then think about which poses let you stretch and strengthen those parts. For example, the breaststroke puts more stress on your upper back and neck from arching up, while the butterfly needs you to extend your mid and lower back.

BREATHING UNDERWATER?

Learning to control, coordinate and extend your breath is very helpful for swimmers. Practice the full yogic breath (page 63) for better control and to slowly improve your lung capacity.

LOVE, ALL

All racquet sports use overhead arm movements, extensions (arm, back and leg reaches) and agility. Whether you're into the thrill of a killer serve or watching a birdie sail silently over the net, try these poses.

- ⊙ Head to toes: Sun salutation (page 58), Triangle pose (page 38)

- ⊙ Arms: Wrist and shoulder rotations (page 73)

- ⊙ Quadriceps: Dancer pose (page 46)

- ⊙ Knees and ankles: Knee and ankle rotations (page 73)

- ⊙ Lower back and hips: From Butterfly pose (page 55), keep your legs still and bend forward with your back straight.

TIGHTNESS BUSTER

To melt away tightness between the shoulders caused by overhead arm movements, try this variation of Cat pose (page 18).

STEP 1: After warming up your spine with Cat pose, return to the neutral position (step 1).

STEP 2: Turn your right hand palm up and place it on the floor under your chest.

STEP 3: Breathe out, sliding your hand along the floor through the space between your left hand and your knees. Rest your right shoulder and the right side of your head on the floor.

STEP 4: Relax for a few breaths, feeling the stretch through your shoulders and between your shoulder blades.

STEP 5: Breathe in, getting back to neutral position. Repeat on the other side.

IRON FISTS, PIROUETTES AND BACK FLIPS

The grace and precision you want in martial arts, dance and gymnastics comes from a lot of practice and from strength and flexibility. Perfect kicks, deep horse stances and the splits require hip and leg flexibility and strength.

- All-over warm-up: Sun salutation (page 58)

- Balance and poise: Tree pose (page 24), Twisting squat pose (page 40), Balancing stick pose (page 44), Dancer pose (page 46)

- Strength: Warrior pose (page 42), Triangle pose (page 38)

- Hip flexibility: Rowing the boat pose (page 16), Swaying palm tree pose (page 20), Butterfly pose (page 55)

- Kicking speed: Knee rotations (page 73), Forward bend pose (page 34), Playful lion pose (page 53)

For graceful arms that move at the speed of light, you need strong and flexible shoulders, biceps and triceps. Try this variation of Cat pose (page 18).

STEP 1: Starting in neutral position (step 1), pretend you're a cat lapping up milk. Breathe in, using your arms to dip your face down to the floor.

STEP 2: Breathe out, pushing back up again. Keep your elbows close to your body and your spine moving smoothly.

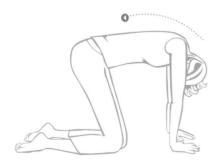

Repeat up to 20 times.

SHE HASN'T MOVED IN HOURS

Believe it or not, sitting still for hours at a time is hard on a body. When we sit at a desk, play on a computer, watch TV or go to the movies, we often slouch, which puts a lot of pressure on our spines.

RULE #1: Try to keep your abdominal muscles lightly contracted, or pulled in, and your chest lifted. This keeps your back straight.

RULE #2: The human body functions better with some regular movement. You can do the following simple stretches in your chair.

NECK STRETCHES

Do these gently and with control.

STEP 1: Breathe in, dropping your chin to your chest.

STEP 2: Breathe out, lifting your chin up to the sky. Don't crunch your neck by dropping your head back.

STEP 3: Breathe in, bringing your head back to center. Breathe out, bringing your right ear toward your right shoulder.

STEP 4: Breathe in, bringing your head back to center. Breathe out, bringing your left ear toward your left shoulder.

STEP 5: Breathe in, bringing your head back to center. Breathe out, turning your head to the right to look over your right shoulder.

STEP 6: Breathe in, bringing your head back to center. Breathe out, turning your head to the left to look over your left shoulder.

STEP 7: Breathe in, bringing your head back to center.

Repeat 10 times.

SEATED ARM, SHOULDER AND BACK STRETCH

STEP 1: Reach up to the sky with the fingertips of one hand while you reach down to the ground with the fingertips of your other hand. Take a few breaths as you reach.

STEP 2: Change arms to reach in the opposite directions. Take a few breaths.

Repeat five times.

SEATED TWIST

STEP 1: Breathe in, placing your left hand on the outside of your right knee and your right hand behind you.

STEP 2: Breathe out, turning your torso, shoulders, neck and head to your right to look over your shoulder.

STEP 3: Hold the twist for a few breaths and then breathe in to come back to the center.

Repeat on the opposite side.

YOGA FOR WHAT AILS YOU

Yoga has been used for thousands of years as therapy to treat all kinds of health problems. We're not the first generation on the planet to feel tired or stressed out. Here are a few complaints that can creep up on you and the yoga that may help. See if they make a difference for you. But remember, these are *not* a substitute for medical care.

FATIGUE

Being physically tired doesn't mean it's time to drink some caffeinated soda. It's actually a strong message from your body that shouldn't be ignored. Have you been doing too much lately? Are you sleeping too little?

POSES: Slow and gentle Sun salutation (page 58), Swaying palm tree pose (page 20), Corpse pose (page 30)

BREATHING: Alternate nostril pranayama (page 64)

Also try the Outer eyes closed, inner eyes open relaxation (page 66). Don't worry if you fall asleep — you probably need it. Just make sure you're covered up.

Before you start, think about what you want your yoga to do for you. Focus on that to get even more out of the poses.

80

HEADACHE

If you get a headache every once in a while, it could be from eyestrain or dehydration. Are you spending too much time in front of the TV or glued to the computer? Are you drinking enough water?

POSES: Joint rotations (page 73), Swaying palm tree pose (page 20)

BREATHING: Alternate nostril pranayama (page 64)

Also try Corpse pose (page 30) in a dark and quiet room with an eye pillow over your eyes.

NERVOUSNESS

People get nervous for lots of reasons — some real and some imagined. And the worst thing is, feeling nervous usually doesn't help the situation you are in. Try to stay grounded and calm yourself down enough to see things clearly.

POSES: Slow Sun salutation, concentrating on your breath (page 58), Forward bend pose (page 34), Cobra pose (page 36), Warrior pose (page 42), Corpse pose (page 30)

BREATHING: Alternate nostril pranayama (page 64)

Also try Outer eyes closed, inner eyes open relaxation (page 66). Clear your mind and visualize yourself feeling confident and capable. A solution might come to you or you might realize you have nothing to worry about.

CRAMPS

Sadly, cramps are a fact of life for lots of girls when they get their period. The good news is that there are things you can try that can really help. If you feel up to it, do yoga while you have your period, but don't overdo it and do avoid inversions like Downward facing dog or Bridge pose.

POSES: Cat pose (page 18), Thunderbolt pose (page 28), Corpse pose (page 30)

BREATHING: Abdominal breathing (step 3 from the Full yogic breath pranayama, page 63)

DIY YOGINI

It's easy to add to your yoga practice and feel like a pro with some simple accessories you've made yourself.

Walking into a busy yoga studio, you'll see lots of yogis and yoginis with their mats easily slung over their shoulders in a simple but hugely practical invention called a yoga mat bag. Make one to measure and toting your mat around will become second nature.

During relaxation at the end of a class, your yoga teacher might place a magical little pillow over your eyes. Two seconds later you're off in la-la land. It takes only a few simple steps and the right materials to make your very own pillow.

Both projects involve sewing and are very easy, but if you don't have experience with sewing, check out a book on sewing basics.

These projects can be sewn by hand but will be faster on a machine. Ask for help from an adult.

Never forget that a little luxury is something that no hardworking yogini should do without, and getting a massage is just the ticket. Find a friend and follow the instructions to pamper each other with a simple hand, head and foot massage.

Yoga mat bag

A mat bag is the perfect accessory to keep your yoga mat clean and easy to tote around.

GET IT FIRST

- ⊙ durable cotton fabric (see instructions to figure out how much you'll need)

- ⊙ braided cord 1 cm (1/2 in.) thick

- ⊙ a safety pin

- ⊙ an iron and ironing board

- ⊙ measuring tape, scissors, thread to match the fabric, pins, a needle or sewing machine.

STEP 1: Measure your rolled yoga mat to find its length and circumference (its size around).

STEP 2: Add 15 cm (6 in.) to the length and 9 cm (3½ in.) to the circumference. Cut a rectangle using these dimensions. If the fabric frays, run a zigzag or overcast stitch around the edges before continuing.

STEP 3: Lay the fabric right sides (the sides that will show) down. Fold the long edges over 1.5 cm (3/4 in.) and press with an iron.

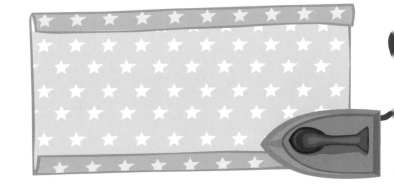

STEP 4: Fold and pin a short edge over 4 cm (1½ in.). Sew a line of straight stitches 0.5 cm (¼ in.) in from the cut edge, removing the pins as you sew. Repeat another line of stitches 0.5 cm (¼ in.) in from the first to reinforce it. This makes a channel for the drawstring.

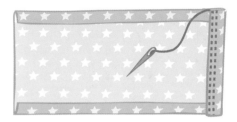

STEP 5: Using the measurements from step 2, double the length of the bag and add its width. Cut the cord this length. Knot each end. Attach a safety pin to one end and feed the cord through the channel. Turn the fabric right side up. Stitch each end of the cord to the bottom corners of the fabric. Have the ends sticking off the edge of the fabric.

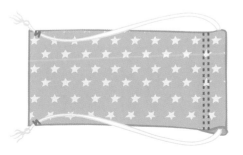

STEP 6: Fold the fabric in half as shown, and pin the bottom and sides of the bag together. (The cord should be on the inside and the knotted ends sticking out.) Sew the fabric together 1 cm (½ in.) from the edge, removing the pins as you go. Sew to just below the drawstring channel.

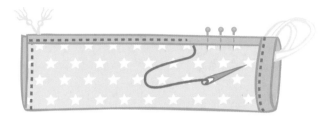

STEP 7: Turn the bag right side out, slide in your yoga mat and away you go!

X-TRAS

⊙ Sew on a little pocket to keep your jewelry, sunglasses and other stuff safe while you're getting your "OM" on.

⊙ Decorate your mat bag to your heart's content with fabric markers, paint, beads, appliqué — whatever you like. Let your creativity shine.

Relaxation eye pillow

So easy to make, an eye pillow is the perfect companion for relaxation practices. It darkens a room in an instant, and the sweet-smelling lavender makes you feel peaceful. (If you're making the pillow as a gift, be sure your friend isn't allergic to the scent or the filling.) Try putting your pillow in the freezer for an hour before you use it to relieve headaches. Or warm it up by rubbing it between your hands to release the scent — then drift away.

GET IT FIRST

- 125 mL ($^1/_2$ c.) dried lavender flowers
- 250 mL (1 c.) flax seeds (you can substitute small beans or rice if allergies are an issue)
- two 20 cm x 15 cm (8 in. x 6 in.) pieces of soft, smooth fabric (brushed cotton or silk works well)
- a medium-size funnel, a measuring cup, a bowl and spoon
- measuring tape, scissors, pins, thread to match the fabric, a needle or sewing machine

STEP 1: If the fabric is fraying, run a zigzag or overcast stitch around the edges before starting.

STEP 2: Pin the right sides of the fabric (the sides that will show) together so the edges are even, but leave a 4 cm (1$^1/_2$ in.) opening on one short side.

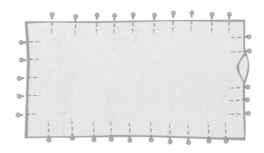

STEP 3: Sew the pieces together 1 cm (¹/₂ in.) from the edges, removing the pins as you go. Make sure you don't sew the opening closed!

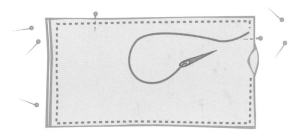

STEP 6: Pin the opening closed, tucking in the extra fabric. Hand sew the pillow closed, removing the pins as you go.

STEP 4: Carefully turn the pillow right side out.

STEP 5: Stir the dried lavender flowers and flax seeds together. Using the funnel, pour them into the pillow.

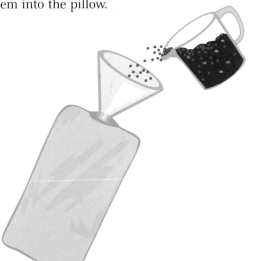

X-TRAS

⊙ You can get fancy and decorate the pillow, but decorate one side only. You don't want to irritate the tender skin around your eyes.

At-home massage therapy

Massage is a real-life demo of how the physical, mental and emotional sides of you are all connected. And you and your yogini friends get to enjoy a little luxury at the same time. Mental stress and emotional problems can cause physical tension in the body, so it just makes sense that massaging tense muscles can relax your mind and calm your emotions.

The type of oil and amount of pressure you use (how hard you press) will depend on the kind of massage you want to give. Here are some guidelines, but experiment to see what works for you.

⊙ Soothing and warming massage: sesame or almond oil; gentle pressure and smooth strokes

⊙ Relaxing and cooling massage: coconut or olive oil; gentle pressure and a variety of strokes

⊙ Invigorating and heating massage: very little sunflower, mustard or sesame oil; firm pressure and a variety of strokes

As you take turns giving each other massages, keep communicating. Make sure your friend is comfortable and okay with the pressure you are using, and when you're the one being massaged, let your friend know how you're feeling.

CAUTION!

If you have allergies (especially to nuts), ask at your health food store for a recommendation for an oil that is safe for you. And always spot-test for allergic reactions by putting a drop of the oil on your wrist and covering it with a bandage. Twelve hours later, check to see whether you have a reaction such as itchiness or red marks. If you do, wash the area with cool water and don't use this kind of oil.

Don't give or get a massage if you aren't feeling well.

PREP TIME

Cover the ground with old towels, sheets or blankets to make your friend comfortable and to catch oil drips and spills (they will happen). Keep a damp cloth and paper towels handy for more extreme spills, and extra towels or blankets in case your friend feels cold.

Have your friend lie on her back. Putting a folded towel under her head and a bolster under her knees is a nice touch. If lying down isn't an option, she can also sit in a comfy chair that you can easily move around.

These simple head, hand and foot massages are the perfect way to help melt away tension. It will be especially relaxing for your friend if you warm up the oil a bit in your hands as you use it.

HEAD

We're using our brains every second of the day. A relaxing head massage dissolves mental tension. Before beginning, make sure your friend's hair is loose and tangle-free.

STEP 1: Put a few drops of oil on the top of her forehead.

STEP 2: Use your fingers to make small, crisscrossing lines from one ear across her hairline to the other ear.

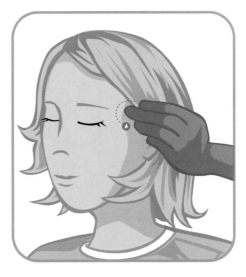

STEP 3: Starting at her hairline, move your fingers in little circles from the center of her forehead out to her temples. Gently turn her head to each side to continue massaging the back of her head.

STEP 4: Using feedback from your friend, come up with other strokes that feel good. Respect your friend's neck by making sure you don't lift her head or pull on it.

STEP 5: Finish with a few soothing strokes over her whole head using your whole hand.

Hands

Think about how much you use your hands in a day and you'll see why they deserve some special attention. Work on one hand first, then the other.

STEP 1: Pour a few drops of oil into your hands. Holding your friend's hand with both of yours, make circles over her wrist bones with your fingers and thumbs.

STEP 2: Make smooth strokes down the back of her hand with your thumbs.

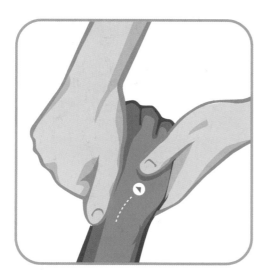

STEP 3: Hold her hand in one of yours and gently squeeze each finger from the base to the fingertip with the thumb and index finger of your other hand. Make little circles over the joints.

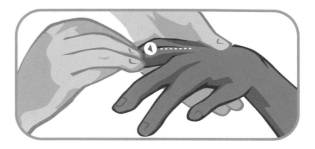

STEP 4: Turn her hand over, still holding it in your hand. Using your other hand, stroke from the base of her palm toward the fingertips 5 to 10 times.

STEP 5: Finish by covering your friend's hand with both of yours and slowly drawing your hands away, letting her hand gently rest on the towel. Repeat three times.

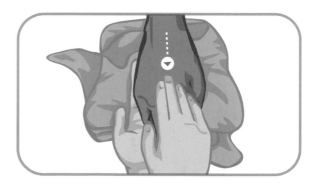

FEET

If you're short on time, go straight to the feet because a foot massage is relaxation guaranteed. Massage one foot and then the other using confident and firm strokes so you don't tickle your friend.

STEP 1: Cup your friend's ankle with your palms and move your hands in small circles in one direction and then in the other.

STEP 2: With your thumbs, rub the top of her foot with long, smooth strokes.

STEP 3: Hold her foot in one hand and gently squeeze and rub each of her toes with the thumb and index finger of your other hand. Stretch her toes by very gently pulling them toward you.

STEP 4: Use your knuckles to gently knead from the ball of her foot down the arch to her heel.

STEP 5: Using long, smooth strokes, make a T-shape with your thumbs by moving up the middle of the sole and out across the ball of her foot.

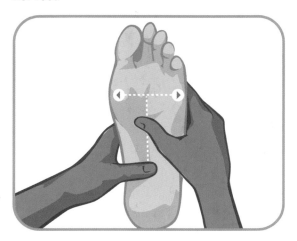

STEP 6: Finish by covering her foot with both your hands and slowly drawing them away.

A foot massage can sweeten your sleep, and it's easy to do for yourself before bed. Slip socks on after the massage to keep your feet warm and your sheets clean.

FINISHING TOUCHES

Gently wipe away any extra oil with a towel. Make sure your friend is warm enough while she lies there until she's ready to face the world again.

STYLES OF YOGA: What's your flavor?

Hatha yoga, the kind of yoga that focuses on the physical body, has been around for a long time, so many different people have had a chance to put their spin on it. All the different physical styles of yoga are based on Hatha, so it's a great place to start. In a Hatha class you can expect static poses (where you hold one pose for several breaths), yogic flows (where you move dynamically from one pose to the next in time with your breathing), breathing, meditation and relaxation.

Here's a rough guide to several of the other major types of yoga. Keep in mind that they all share the basic philosophy of trying to find that union between body, mind and breath.

ASHTANGA YOGA

Also called Power yoga, this is the most physically demanding of the styles and not really for beginners. You build strength, flexibility and stamina by jumping from one pose to another and by using a special way of breathing. It was developed by Pattabhi Jois.

BIKRAM YOGA

Also called Hot yoga, it's exactly that. The room is heated to 30 to 40°C (85 to 100°F), so get ready to sweat. All classes follow the same 26 poses and last for an hour and a half. It's intense and therefore not ideal for beginners. Developed by Bikram Choudhury, it's designed to cleanse you from the inside out.

IYENGAR YOGA

This style focuses on proper alignment — making sure your body is in exactly the right position — so you'll hold the postures longer than in other classes. It's where to go to use yoga props and is good for beginners. It was developed by B.K.S. Iyengar.

90°

There are many other styles of yoga to check out, depending on where you live, what's available and what you are looking for. Don't be shy — yoga teachers are a great source of info and are always happy to explain the style of yoga they teach.

WHERE TO GO TO FIND OUT MORE ...

This book is only the tip of the yoga iceberg. There's so much more waiting for you to learn. Curious?

For more info on yoga poses, yogic philosophy, massage and more, there are lots of magazines, books and Web sites. Focus your search by surfing the Web and then hit your local library or bookstore.

If you're looking for classes, ask your phys ed teacher, coach or friends. Word of mouth is a great way to find a good studio. If you're a groundbreaker and don't know anyone else into yoga, check out the Web, your local newspaper, community and recreation centers or even the phone book. More classes are available than ever before, so it should be pretty easy to find one that suits your body and schedule.

Not every style of yoga works for everyone. Or you may not be comfortable with the instructor who's teaching the class. Use what you've learned in your practice so far to listen to yourself and decide whether something works for you. Keep asking yourself questions, and check with the experts if you're unsure.

Glossary

Asana (AH-sah-nah): the Sanskrit word for "seat," it is a pose or position that makes a place for the energy in your body to settle

Chakra (CHAH-krah): the Sanskrit word for "spinning disk," it is a place where two or more energy channels cross in the body. There are seven main ones located along the spinal channel

Dynamic pose: a pose where you keep moving in and out of the full stretch

Extension: when part of your body reaches beyond its normal range of motion

Guru (GOO-roo): a master teacher. The Sanskrit translation explains it as someone who leads you from the darkness to the light, or in other words, from ignorance to knowledge

Hatha (HA-thah) yoga: the branch of yoga that uses the physical body to achieve union between the body, mind and breath. *Hatha* comes from the Sanskrit words for sun and moon union, symbolizing the balancing of two opposite kinds of energy

Inversion: a pose where your hips are higher than your head

Mantra (MAHN-trah): words or sounds that are chanted either out loud or in your head to focus your mind and affect your mood and energy. In yoga the words are usually in Sanskrit but can be in any language

Meditation: a practice to quiet the mind and reach an internal stillness

Mudra (MOO-drah): a head, foot or hand position that redirects energy in your body, affecting your mood or attitude

Prana (PRAH-nah): life force energy, the same as qi (chi) in Chinese martial arts

Pranayama (prah-nah-yah-mah): special breathing techniques that are used to affect your life force energy, or prana

Relaxation pose: a pose where your physical body is relaxed or held in such a way to relax your nervous system

Sanskrit: an ancient language from India. It is known to be an incantational language, where the sounds of the words actually have a special energy

Strength pose: a strength-building pose that makes you really use your muscles

Visualization: the practice of picturing images in your head

Yoga (yoh-gah): the Sanskrit word for yoke, meaning the union, or the bringing and holding together of different things (in this case body, mind and breath)

Yogini (yoh-ghee-nee): a girl who practices yoga. A yogi is the boy version

Index